SPIRITUALITY FOR EVERYDAY LIVING

Brian C. Taylor

THE LITURGICAL PRESS
Collegeville, Minnesota 56321

Cover by Joshua Jeide, O.S.B.

ISBN 13: 978-0-8146-1757-1
ISBN 10: 0-8146-1757-3

12 13 14 15 16 17 18

Library of Congress Cataloging-in-Publication Data

Taylor, Brian C., 1951–
    Spirituality for everyday living : an adaptation of the Rule of
St. Benedict / Brian C. Taylor.
        p.   cm.
    Includes bibliographical references.
    ISBN 0-8146-1757-3
    1. Spiritual life—Anglican authors.   2. Benedict, Saint, Abbot of
Monte Cassino.   Regula.   I. Title.
BV4501. T27   1989
255' .106—dc19
Shared Cataloging for DNLM   89-2261
Library of Congress   CIP

Contents

Preface

This book was written to be a guide for reflecting in a practical way upon the spiritual life as it is found in everyday experience. It is based on *The Rule of St. Benedict* and the Benedictine tradition. If used in a group setting, one section should be read before each session by all participants, together with the accompanying readings in *The Rule of St. Benedict*[1] and the meditations. The group would then talk about how each element of the *Rule*, in turn, can be lived out in one's life. Ideally, the chapters should be considered with perhaps a week between each one. Alternatively, one could consider them together, as in a retreat format. This text may also be used as an individual guide for self-reflection, using the section-by-section process.

My own interest in the Benedictine way stems from yearly retreats at Christ in the Desert Benedictine Monastery near my home in New Mexico. As I found a sense of *simpatico* with the style and content of the spirituality of the

1. For the readings in *The Rule of St. Benedict*, I recommend one of the inexpensive paperback versions: *The Rule of St. Benedict in English*, ed. Timothy Fry (Collegeville: The Liturgical Press, 1982), or *St. Benedict's Rule for Monasteries*, trans. Leonard J. Doyle (Collegeville: The Liturgical Press, 1948).

brothers, I began to study both *The Rule of St. Benedict* and writings on Benedictinism. I quickly began to see that here was a spirituality that made me feel as if I had arrived ''home.'' In the winter of 1987 I took the opportunity of enrolling in a weeklong tutorial with Esther de Waal at the Church Divinity School of the Pacific in Berkeley, California. As I read each day and we discussed particular issues of the *Rule* in daily ordinary living, we found that the central themes of the *Rule* lead one back inevitably to the central themes of being human: commitment, balance, and being in relationship with God, others, material possessions, and the world. These are issues that directly affect each one of us. As a result, the idea grew up of producing some kind of text that would make St. Benedict's practical wisdom more accessible to men and women of today who are involved in relationships, careers, family, community, and parish life.

St. Benedict lived and developed his *Rule* for monasteries around fifteen hundred years ago. Abbot to twelve monasteries, he intended this writing to be only for those over whom he exercised authority. The eventual widespread use of *The Rule of St. Benedict* in hundreds of monasteries throughout Europe in the High Middle Ages was completely unforeseen by its author. Speaking to his monks of the sixth century and therefore to a completely different world from ours in many ways, Benedict at times seems strange, even arcane. And yet, through the filter of history and culture comes an eternal message. As humanity developed through the Middle Ages, the Renaissance, and right up to our own postnuclear age, the message of Benedict has remained, yet has constantly evolved in its expression. Benedictine communities have consistently lived out this sixth century message in ways appropriate to each generation: through manual labor, keeping the lamp of education lit during the Dark Ages, illuminating manuscripts and writing books, composing chant and folk music, advising monarchs and praying in cloistered isolation, running cathedrals, speaking out on social issues, leading workshops, and, above all, providing witness to the life of prayer lived in human community.

The message given in the sixth century continues to speak to humanity today. Issues of living in the late twentieth-century world are wisely addressed and practical advice is given. It is my heartfelt hope that others will find affirmation and challenge for their everyday lives through the spirit of Benedict and Benedictinism.

All quotes from *The Rule of St. Benedict* itself are taken from *The Rule of St. Benedict 1980*, ed. Timothy Fry (Collegeville, Minn.: The Liturgical Press, 1981).

All quotes from the Bible are taken from the Revised Standard Version.

My deepest thanks go to my family, Esther de Waal, the community of Christ in the Desert, Pepper Marts, Jack Schanaar, and the "Wednesday Morning Group" at the San Isidro community.

Introduction

The motivation for this adaptation of *The Rule of St. Benedict* for everyday living was a desire for spiritual survival. I am a married Episcopal priest with two young children and a busy twentieth-century job and mortgage who is very much in the world (but, I hope, not too very much *of* it).

Over the years I have had to do quite a bit of soul searching when I read either classic or modern authors on the spiritual life. How much can I adapt to my lifestyle? In what ways is the life of prayer being described simply impossible, given my situation? Am I really not "making the grade" spiritually as long as I insist on keeping my job, marriage, and family intact with the necessary long hours of attention that requires? Was Thomas Merton right when he said that in the monastery one found "Christianity in its most perfect form"?

Somehow I maintained a nagging sense that the God who had called me into this particular life would use this very life to draw me into a deeply faith-filled life. Why would God call me into a lifestyle that the vast majority of humanity has always lived and then say that there is some other, "better" way of faith? And yet it is difficult to find good writing on the subject of an "everyday" spirituality. Out of a

11

need to survive spiritually, therefore, I would translate for my own use what was written for a much different lifestyle. I would also hope for the emergence of some tradition, some structure that could provide me the same kind of vehicle for committed growth in grace that the monastic life provides for monks.

The Rule of St. Benedict is the vehicle that emerged, and I continue to translate. The irony is that it was the monastic witness that provided me with a "way," an approach that could directly inform my spiritual life in the world. The Rule seems itself almost written for living "in the world," even though its original intent was for Benedict's monastery. Some scholars feel that Benedict was simply describing the essentials of a Christian life, normative for all but expressed through the particularities of the monastery. The Rule, as Cardinal Basil Hume states, "makes it possible for ordinary folk to live lives of quite extraordinary value."[1] There are no heroics here, no spectacular feats of spiritual accomplishment—just a steady and committed focus on God through the vehicles of prayer, labor, relationships, and study. Through the development of attitudes about such ordinary things as money, possessions, time, authority, and food, the monk (and the man or woman "in the world") is radically transformed by grace.

To live according to a tradition and under a rule of life, whether Benedict's or someone else's, is to enter consciously into a process of growth in grace and to undertake a specific discipline used in that process. However, a rule of life is not undertaken for its own sake, so that one can "become disciplined," as if that were a primary virtue. The need for order can be an extremely neurotic form of self-control when it is no longer a means to reach God but, rather, an end in itself. The discipline of a rule of life is undertaken as a means to freedom in God. "St. Benedict, in legislating for everything from consultative processes to wine-

1. Basil Hume, In Praise of Benedict (London: Hodder and Stoughton, 1981) 34.

consumption, from kitchen arrangements to modes of punishment, does so in the belief that a well-ordered human community is more conducive to holiness than a badly organized one."[2] Why is this? It is, to my mind, because in ordering one's life according to a form of spirituality that thousands of people have lived with and found freedom in for fifteen hundred years, one has a better chance of growing in grace than through any lifestyle one could dream up on one's own.

Benedict of Nursia wrote a *Rule* of life that partly adapted existing rules for monks. His originality was in creating a lifestyle that demanded one's all and yet recognized human weakness. He asked for a holy singlemindedness to be lived out through balance and moderation. "Therefore we intend to establish a school for the Lord's service. In drawing up its regulations, we hope to set down nothing harsh, nothing burdensome. The good of all concerned, however, may prompt us to a little strictness in order to amend faults and to safeguard love."[3]

Balance, zeal, and moderation are the qualities of *The Rule of St. Benedict* that make it a humane approach for imperfect human beings who seek the perfection of God in their lives. In this sense, Benedict's *Rule* is incarnational—it works with people as they are in this world, calling them to what they can become in Christ. While the Franciscan way is a revolutionary, transforming force that acts on society from without, the Benedictine way is a force from within that acts as leaven in the loaf. To become fully human in this life as it has been given us is to allow the sacredness of the ordinary to become manifest. To seek God in work, cooking, prayer, community, greeting strangers, and dealing with possessions is to enter into the mystery of the incarnation. Benedict did not add to the Gospel of Jesus

2. Dominic Milroy, "Education According to The Rule of St. Benedict," *Ampleforth Journal,* no. 84 (Autumn 1979) 2.
3. *The Rule of St. Benedict 1980* (henceforth *RB*) ed. Timothy Fry (Collegeville: The Liturgical Press, 1981) Prologue 45-47.

Christ. He simply provided a way of seeing Christ's continual incarnation in this world.

It is these qualities that commend *The Rule of St. Benedict* to ordinary folk like me. "St. Benedict's idea was to form a community of monks bound to live together until death, under rule, in common life, in the monastery of their profession, as a religious family, leading a life not of marked austerity but devoted to the service of God; the service consisting in the community act of the celebration of the divine office, and in the discipline of a life of ordered manual work and religious reading, according to the *Rule* and under obedience to the abbot."[4] I hope in this writing to see how that life can be translated outside the monastery to the place where most of us live.

Readings in The Rule of St. Benedict: Read through the entire *Rule* to gain a general overview.

4. Cuthbert Butler, Benedictine Monachism (London: Longmans, Green and Co., 1924) 33.

1

Commitment to Life—Stability, *Conversatio*, and Obedience

INTRODUCTION

Monastic life is grounded in commitment. This is expressed through formal vows, which, in many traditions, are identified and outlined quite clearly. Benedict did not really do this. The closest thing we have to an outline of Benedictine vows is in chapter 58 of *The Rule of St. Benedict*, wherein it is simply said that a new monk is to promise stability, *conversatio*, and obedience. This is drawn up in a document in the presence of the other monks, signed, and laid on the altar. Aside from this chapter, the vows are dealt with in context, as they apply to any given situation. The three vows are used interchangeably at times, or one or two are mentioned without the others.

What this points to is the fact that underlying the three vows is one commitment. The promise the new monk signs at the altar is one promise, not three. It is a promise to commit one's entire being to the life God has given (stability),

15

to change and grow in grace in this life *(conversatio)* according to the freeing demands and limits this life brings (obedience). Without change and growth, stability is a prison. Without stability, change is chaos. Without mutual commitment, obedience is slavery. And without obedience to a higher authority, change is capricious. It is one life that Benedict proposes, and it is expressed through three facets.

The Benedictine vows provide a way of living life in a balanced tension in the midst of paradox: obedience to the process of change and growth within the context of unchanging commitment. All religious truth is filled with paradox, yet one of the most difficult things for humans to do is to live within its tension. We must choose the other side of the paradox even while in the midst of its opposite. For example, we value children, even treasure them, yet, when we are reading a gripping novel their interruptions become a challenge, a source of dynamic tension. We tend to think a balanced life means one in which there is no tension—a perfectly placid existence. But, in fact, it is quite the opposite. A truly balanced life, if it is to embrace the paradox of truth, is one which *is* in tension: not destructive and stressful but healthy and dynamic. To choose to enter into this tension is to be obedient to the life we have been given. On a theological level, we live in the tension of paradox all the time. Consider the Trinity: God the Father, who is unchanging and eternal (stability) is also unpredictable, in constant motion in the form of Spirit *(conversatio)*. The Son reveals perfect *obedience* to both eternal truth and creative dynamism. Yet the three Persons of the Trinity are one. So it is with the Benedictine vow, which embraces three seemingly paradoxical facets in order to be complete. Dynamic balance is found in obedience to a lifelong commitment to a group of people while one is also fully committed to change.

With this in mind, we now turn to examine each facet as it finds expression in our lives.

STABILITY

The vow of stability is the promise a monk makes to remain in the monastic community of profession for life. It is a laying down of one's life in its entirety, placing it in the hands of God. The vow of stability is the first of the vows because nothing is possible until we give over our entire life to the primacy of God's kingdom. If we leave ourselves an escape hatch we have one foot out the door, and we are not fully committed. If we say to ourselves that we will stay committed as long as commitment stays exciting and devoid of suffering, we are not fully committed.

The Benedictine vow of stability is a vow to a community of people rather than to a place. In this sense it is a marriage, by which the members of the monastic family bind themselves to each other for life. Such a vow is directly translatable to any relationship of love, but especially to family love. To be a husband, daughter, mother, brother or wife is to live in a lifelong relationship with others. But as long as we keep even one opening in the back of our mind, we cannot reap the benefits of a fully committed love relationship. We will always be only partly "there."

Because Benedict recognized the primacy of stable and committed love, the vow of stability finds expression throughout *The Rule of St. Benedict* in his attitude towards relationships. The grass is not greener "over there": one must work out one's problems with *this* person because, if one doesn't, one will have to work it out with *that* person. This is precisely what is so freeing about the vow of stability, both in monastic and family life. To have to work it out is to demand growth, as painful as it is, and that is freeing. Faithfulness is a limit that forces us to stop running and encounter God, self, and other right now, right here.

Without this ultimate commitment to the other monks, to wife or husband, to child or parent, change is difficult at best because it lives under the threat of abandonment.

With a commitment to stability, change is no longer a threat but something to be undertaken together. One can change or ask for change in the other when one knows that one is loved and that this request will not drive the other away. This is tremendously liberating, and Benedict knew this about families, about monks, about people. Judgment is hard, but it brings healing.

Within the stable, committed environment of monastery or family, life is not, of course, all a happy process of liberation. The vow of stability does not guarantee happiness any more than a marriage partner can. "It is all too easy to idealize both marriage and the monastic community as institutions which can be the panacea for so many of the ills of contemporary society. People hoping to escape the overwhelming isolation and loneliness which is so near the surface today . . . believe that either marriage or some form of common life provides the answer."[1] While this may be true, it is by no means automatically so. Both the marriage bond and the monastic vows involve commitment to years of difficult, often painful learning. Neither guarantees automatic peace of mind. But each gives a permanent, secure context in which to enter into the inevitable difficulties of growth, for we know that growth will indeed come through commitment. "Never swerving from his instructions, then, but faithfully observing his teaching in the monastery until death, we shall through patience share in the sufferings of Christ that we may deserve also to share in his kingdom."[2]

Beyond the challenging and sometimes painful process of growth in a relationship, there is the monotony of stability. One wakes up in a marriage to the same face, year after year. There are the little habits and quirks that never seem to go away. But it is monotony, found in the daily round of either monastic offices or keeping a household go-

1. Esther de Waal, "The Benedictine Tradition and the Family" (unpublished manuscript).
2. *The Rule of St. Benedict 1980*, ed. Timothy Fry (Collegeville: The Liturgical Press, 1981) Prologue 50.

ing, that forces us to stop running away and find God in the here and now. The Cistercian monk Michael Casey said that "the whole purpose of stability is to make provision for an atmosphere of creative monotony in which there is nothing that unnecessarily binds the monk to transitory things."[3] Monotony makes us deal with the things that distraction seeks to avoid. And whatever we avoid will surely come back, once the distraction is over. Benedict spoke of a good kind of zeal with which monks should love one another through the monotony of the years "supporting with the greatest patience one another's weaknesses of body or behavior, and earnestly competing in obedience to one another."[4]

It is the failure to commit oneself entirely that blocks creativity in the spiritual life, in the artistic life, in relational life. Meeting one's obligations with a minimum of commitment may seem like freedom, but it enslaves us to what is fleeting. Both Benedictine and familial vows of stability fly in the face of everything our modern society teaches us. Relationships are disposable, society says, and the message is that "something better out there awaits us." In the instability of our age we are constantly reassessing the self— our direction and purpose, our commitments and values. Without the constancy of stability, this reassessment can create chaos.

Ultimately, the vow of stability is a vow of stability to God. God is the only truly eternal rock upon which we can stand. But God calls us into a particular life, to be spent in the company of particular people: spouse, parents, children, siblings, lifelong friends. Further, we are often called into a particular vocation: teacher, laborer, homemaker, businessman, nurse. To accept one's life as it is given is to begin to find freedom. As we live the vow of stability we

3. Michael Casey, "St. Benedict's Approach to Prayer," *Cistercian Studies* (1980) 339.
4. *RB* 72.5-6.

enter into the mystery of our ordinary lives more deeply and find the divine within.

Readings in The Rule of St. Benedict: chapters 1 and 58

Meditations:

What does Benedict say about those who are "uncommitted"?

What seems to be the benefit of Benedictine stability, according to *The Rule of St. Benedict?*

To whom and to what am I committed for life?

What does that internal commitment do for me and others?

What happens to monk or marriage partner who cannot continue in stability, or who seems to be called out of it? How is grace experienced when failure to be fully committed occurs?

CONVERSATIO

The vow of *conversatio* is the most debated vow in terms of its "real meaning," which is why it is left in its untranslated form in most cases. When translated, it comes out in a variety of ways: conversion of life, the life of a monk, conversion of manners (or behavior), and so on. Because of the variety of interpretations, one often finds a convoluted explanation in place of a simple word or phrase. Thomas Merton, with his usual directness, gets right to the point and comes up with an interpretation that pleases me: "In St. Benedict's mind it is simply a formal commitment to live until death as a fervent monk."[5]

How can we possibly translate this vow into our lives? We do not live as monks. And yet, as we read further in the same article by Merton, "It is the vow to respond to-

5. Thomas Merton, "Conversatio Morum," *Cistercian Studies* (1966) 131.

tally and integrally to the word of Christ, 'Come, follow me' by renouncing all that might impede one in following him untrammelled, all that might obscure one's clarity of intent and confuse one's resolve. It is the vow to obey the voice of God, . . . in order to follow the will of God in all things."[6] Herein we find an interpretation we can use no matter what lifestyle we have been given. *Conversatio* is essentially the vow to do *metanoia* (repenting), the turning away from self-will and the turning toward God's will. In the baptismal liturgy in the *Book of Common Prayer*, it is asked of the candidate, "Whenever you fall into sin, will you repent and return to the Lord?" *Conversatio* is the vow to do just that in our day-to-day existence.

The Prologue of *The Rule of St. Benedict* is ringing in its urgency to awake from sleep today and follow Christ's voice. "Let us get up then, at long last, for the Scriptures rouse us when they say: *It is high time for us to arise from sleep.* Let us open our eyes to the light that comes from God, and our ears to the voice from heaven that every day calls out this charge: *If you hear his voice today, do not harden your hearts.*"[7] Now is the time of salvation, and the choice before us is at hand. This urgency is brought home by Benedict again and again, perhaps most dramatically in his oft-repeated plea to keep death always before our eyes, to remember the account we must one day give. There is an open grave outside the chapel of Christ in the Desert Benedictine Monastery right next to two graves where monks are buried. This reminder, both in the *Rule* and at the monastery, is not for the purpose of instilling guilt and fear but to remind us that now is the hour to live the life we are called to live. Now is the time to forsake spiritual death. Now is the time to turn and choose life.

Benedict is understanding of human weakness, to be sure, but he is uncompromising in his expectation of zeal.

---

6. *Ibid.* 133.
7. *RB* Prologue 8-10.

It is this zeal that permeates the *Rule,* zeal for the process of *conversatio,* which assumes that we are doing our best to progress in perfection in Christ, toward whom we move in our spiritual path. Perhaps because, as Westerners, we live in a workaholic culture, because we are wont to do rather than be, we have compensated by laying great emphasis on salvation by grace and not by works. Salvation, indeed, does come through God's grace, yet one finds many Christians who have no spiritual zeal whatsoever. Feeling saved, loved, and justified in Christ, they feel no compulsion "to work out [their] own salvation in fear and trembling."[8] Christians are often uncomfortable with the Letter of James wherein he says, "Show me your faith apart from your works, and I by my works will show you my faith."[9] There are clearly some expectations that Jesus has, the foremost being that we love God "with all our heart, soul, mind and strength."[10] Benedict echoes this call to zeal with ultimate seriousness: "Your way of acting should be different from the world's way; the love of Christ must come before all else. . . . Day by day remind yourself that you are going to die. Hour by hour keep careful watch over all you do, aware that God's gaze is upon you, wherever you may be. As soon as wrongful thoughts come into your heart, dash them against Christ and disclose them to your spiritual father."[11] We need to recover this sense of zealous conversion of life.

The vow of *conversatio* is at the root of growth in grace for all Christians. We are all called to "take up our cross daily" and follow Christ. It is in community that we find the most challenge in this regard. Other people bring out our selfishness and inadequacies. Other people, in their differentness, demand that we grow beyond our rigid boundaries. Other people confront us with the self that

8. Phillipians 2:12.
9. James 2:18b.
10. Mark 12:30.
11. *RB* 4.20-21, 47-50.

needs to die. When done in love, confrontation effectively brings the chance for healing. This is where *conversatio* meets the loving commitment of stability. This is where God's judgment meets mercy. All humans living in any kind of community desperately need to develop this skill of loving confrontation, given and received as a vehicle for God's healing grace.

When I first was married, I felt as if someone suddenly had installed floor-to-ceiling mirrors, covering every wall. There was nowhere to hide! My true self, so easily hidden until then, was completely transparent to my wife and, therefore, to myself. The demands of family or any kind of community life do the same thing. In that exposure of self we have a choice: we can hide and pretend we are not exposed, like the emperor with his ''new clothes,'' or we can deny our egotistical self and turn toward God, change, and life.

Openness to this process, willingness to be responsive to the judgment of God so often expressed through other people, is the heart of the vow of *conversatio*. Esther de Waal states that *''conversatio* is a dynamic matter: it means continual conversion . . . this process, for the individual as for the family or community, is neither smooth nor continuous. Many of the tensions of family life arise from our failure to face up to the painful and challenging demands of growing and changing.''[12]

To be faithful to *conversatio* is to choose the often painful dynamic of change. In family life this can mean making a fool of oneself and admitting it. This exposure, this nakedness, is often the way God judges us, and it gives us a true picture of just who we are and who we are not. Only after judgment is new life possible. Benedict wisely knew that this is a day-by-day event in our lives, and that it is important enough to warrant being a solemn vow, a basic law of daily life.

12. de Waal, ''The Benedictine Tradition and the Family.''

Readings in The Rule of St. Benedict: Prologue, chapter 4

Meditations:

What sort of death to self is Benedict asking for in his *Rule?*

What does the process of *conversatio* really look like in my life?

When is it most difficult to do the turning involved in *conversatio?*

What enables new life after the old self has been revealed?

Do we ever really change? Do we really become more Christ-like as we follow him? What motivates me to become zealous?

Is fear a healthy motivating factor in the life of faith?

OBEDIENCE

At first glance, the vow of obedience may seem terribly medieval as presented by Benedict for his monastery, and, in a sense, it is. He would have the monks unquestioningly follow the command of the abbot, and if they do not, he would have them punished, even physically. Most of us do not live in such an environment today (except perhaps in the military) and would not choose it. The thought of giving over that kind of unconditional authority to another seems antithetical to our way of living. Several things must be kept in consideration. The time in which Benedict was writing was chaotic. Rome, Gaul, and North Africa had all been sacked, and by 535 the Byzantine conquests had commenced. Quasi-monastic pilgrims wandered during this societal chaos. These individualists are briefly mentioned rather unfavorably in the Prologue of *The Rule of St. Benedict.* Even cenobitic monks (those living in community) tended to reflect the undisciplined instability of their times. What was required in this atmosphere was a rule of life, strictly kept, under the close supervision of a wise and loving abbot.

In the best of circumstances, an abbot was just that: wise and loving. One look at the chapters in *The Rule of St. Benedict* describing an abbot's qualities helps us see how it might be possible to give authority over to such a person. "He must vary with circumstances, threatening and coaxing by turns, stern as a taskmaster, devoted and tender as only a father can be. Above all, he must not show too great concern for the fleeting and temporal things of this world, neglecting or treating lightly the welfare of those entrusted to him."[13] The abbot was to be a combination of holy man, charismatic leader, administrator, pastoral counselor, and father. Indeed, many of the monks were mere children, given over to the monastery to be raised. Given the instability in society outside the monastery, the undisciplined spirituality among the "gyrovagues" (pilgrim wanderers) and even cenobitic monks, and the presence of a benevolent, kind master, one can begin to appreciate the need for complete obedience.

But there is another reason for obedience that transcends historical circumstance. It is the need for humans to be completely, unquestioningly obedient to the will of God. For the monk, the abbot represents Christ's presence on earth and therefore God's will, and the abbot undertakes this role in fear and trembling. The abbot represents an outside authority which transcends the individualist's own self-imposed and often inadequate spiritual system. In the tradition of the monastery's *Rule* and the abbot's inherited wisdom, God's transcendent will has a chance of manifesting itself more clearly than through one's own sense of what seems the right thing to do. "It is love that impels them to pursue everlasting life; . . . They no longer live by their own judgment, giving in to their whims and appetites; rather they walk according to another's decisions and directions."[14]

13. *RB* 2.24, 33.
14. *RB* 5.10, 12.

It is this primacy of God's will over self-will that lies at the heart of the vow of obedience for us as well. We like to think of ourselves as independent people, able to think for ourselves and decide what is best for us. Indeed, God gives us intelligence and judgment to use. But there come times when our own stubbornness and desire are challenged by circumstance and we are left with a choice; we can either go on willfully following what we had set out to do, or we can open ourselves to what has been presented in God's wisdom. If we are to be faithful, we must be humble enough in these circumstances to stand aside and accept the will of God. This is obedience.

But the will of God rarely becomes manifest in a vacuum. Most often, it becomes known through people, traditions, teachings, and institutions. The traditional law/teaching to love one's neighbor is the will of God made manifest through human experience—experience that has taught us the hard way what happens when we do not love our neighbor. We can be obedient to this law/teaching or we can choose our own way and suffer greatly in the process. Every choice we make puts us in particular circumstances with their own need for obedience. To choose to be single means we must be obedient to the rule of caution in intimate relations; if we are disobedient to this, we suffer. To choose to be married means we must be obedient to the vow of faithfulness, and if we disobey this rule we suffer. Any choice brings with it limits and rules to which we must be obedient in order to be fulfilled.

Obedience to God's will as manifested through traditions and teachings is not meant solely to keep us out of trouble. Limits and rules, if they are of God, point the way to life. An artist can only create something beautiful through obedience to the training, practice, and laws of color or movement or sound. And a human being can only become something beautiful through obedience to the will of God. This obedience to the discipline of God's will is our training, and it shapes us into what we are created to be. Obedience is therefore ultimately freeing, for it takes us out of ourselves and demands that we give ourselves to something greater than self. "As we progress in this way of life and in faith, we shall run on the path of God's commandments, our hearts overflowing with the inexpressible delight of love."[15] If I am obedient to the will of God through almsgiving I find that this shapes me into a more generous and loving person. If I am obedient to the will of God through fasting I find that this shapes me into a simpler and more focused person.

Through the centuries mankind has discerned the will of God partly through seeing what works and what doesn't. Justice brings peace, and oppression just as surely brings violent unhappiness. To be fulfilled as human beings, we must humble ourselves to what works for human beings. The freedom to find out for ourselves what works and what doesn't is no freedom at all but rather an imprisonment to the limits of our own imagination and intelligence. "Obedience is not an imposed subservience to an external authority but a condition of inward growth. The monk who is not authentically obedient to his abbot and his brethren will not be a happy monk; the carpenter who is not obedient to the laws of governing joints will make an unreliable table. All disobedience represents, in this sense, the pursuit of an illusory freedom which obstructs the acquisition of real freedom."[16]

A good example of the freedom gained through obedience is found in family life. Children need attention, money has to be gotten, my wife must be listened to even when I feel my resources drained. Obedience to these limits within the discipline of family life brings with it a certain freedom, which is found in love. Love as a father and as a husband is deeper than any I have ever known, and I know that this has been made possible through the count-

15. *RB* Prologue 49.

16. Dominic Milroy, "Education According to The Rule of St. Benedict," *Ampleforth Journal,* no. 84 (Autumn 1979) 4.

less acts of obedience to familial limits that I have made over the years: doing this or that because I know that I have to as a father and as a husband. Love without obedience to these limits and rules is a shallow love, unable to really give except when it feels good to do so.

Obedience to the will of God, then, is choosing to do what is asked of us, knowing that God wants us to be fulfilled and free, for we can be sure that God knows better than we do what we need. To be obedient to the limits inherent in the life we have chosen (or been given) is to fully accept our own path. Without obedience, we have one foot on the path we walk and another off of it. But with obedience, we enter fully into the life we live, even into the sometimes unpleasant and obligatory areas that are there for our own good.

At this point in my life, in addition to the rules inherent in family life and in the priesthood, I am trying to be obedient to *The Rule of St. Benedict*. This means doing certain things I do not feel like doing at times. It means saying an office, even when I feel I should be off doing something "important." It means thinking twice about whether or not I really need that enticing purchase. It means balancing my social life with solitude, even when I am frightened of silence. I go against my immediate feelings and am obedient to this exterior authority in my life for one reason: I have found that through the limits of obedience I grow beyond the confines of the self with its desires and its traps. Through obedience to the *Rule*, I have found myself obedient in some measure to the will of God.

Readings in The Rule of St. Benedict: chapters 2, 5, 64, 71

Meditations:

In the life I live, what rules are inherent?

What happens to me when I am disobedient to those rules?

Why does my ego rebel against obedience?

In what way is God's will made known to me?

How does growth through obedience differ from trying to earn our way into heaven by our own righteous efforts?

2

Life in Balance—
Prayer, Study, and Work

INTRODUCTION

In his *Rule,* Benedict very carefully worked out a daily regimen of activity designed to produce growth through wholeness. The three activities of the monk are prayer, study, and work: the polarities of spirit, mind, and body. This balance in daily living was strictly adhered to, for Benedict knew that if we were to follow our "natural" tendencies we would be unbalanced in some way or other. Perhaps because most of us follow our impulses, or perhaps because of the necessities of job schedules, which monks do not share, we find ourselves out of balance in this regard. While a perfectly balanced day of prayer, manual work, and learning through study may not be possible for us, we can nonetheless seek a measure of this balance. Those of us who work with our minds require exercise on a regular basis, or physical labor around the house. Those who make a living doing manual labor must find ways of stimulating the mind. All of us need to find ways of introducing prayer into our overworked lives. Without a balance of activities, we cannot become whole, as we are made to be as humans.

Benedict assumes that the monk will pursue these activities with singlemindedness and zeal, as we must. "He wants no half-measure in the spiritual life. There is in him a kind of compulsion, a drive for absoluteness. In his view life is not worth living unless it strives for the perfection of love. In this he is uncompromising and does not yield until unity of purpose and resolve has been achieved; . . . he wants his disciples to give all on earth, in order to gain all in heaven."[1]

In a previous section, it was pointed out how desperately this zeal is needed in the life of faith. Conversion of life is no casual thing. However, Benedict has a way of making zeal humane through his parallel attitude of moderation: "In drawing up its regulations, we hope to set down nothing harsh, nothing burdensome."[2] Indeed, when dealing with the elderly, ill, weak or young in the monastery, Benedict strongly advises that the *Rule* be bent and softened in places. When legislating food and drink, he indicates that an absence of wine and only one type of dish would be best, but given the weakness of monks, that a certain amount of wine and two dishes be offered. When a *Rule* for living the Gospel, Benedict's or anyone else's, becomes law, it has become an obstacle to grace, not a vehicle of it. Jesus reminds us of this: "The sabbath was made for man, not man for the sabbath."[3] In a humorous passage, Benedict displays his knowledge that ultimately the *Rule* is made for man, not the other way around. After a very detailed chapter on the order of psalmody for the various offices, he advises, "Above all else we urge that if anyone finds this distribution of the psalms unsatisfactory, he should arrange whatever he judges better."[4]

1. Guy-Marie Oury, *St. Benedict, Blessed by God* (Collegeville: The Liturgical Press, 1980) 19.

2. *The Rule of St. Benedict 1980*, ed. Timothy Fry (Collegeville: The Liturgical Press, 1981) Prologue 46.

3. Mark 2:27.

4. *RB* 18.22.

It is this paradoxical attitude of zealous moderation that defines the uniqueness of Benedictine life. Such an attitude draws us forward into our calling in Christ, yet recognizes our human frailty. Such an attitude allows us to be ordinary humans engaged in the extraordinary venture of life in God. "Perhaps that might sound as a strange contribution to make to the Church—to be witnesses to normalcy—but maybe, in a day such as this, a witness to balance is the most needed."[5] It is an ordinary, normal life that uses all to glorify God: the spirit to open the heart to grace, the body to accomplish work, and the mind to increase knowledge. Through the medium of ordinary balanced living, Benedict expects that one will find God. Through both zeal and moderation, the ordinary is transformed into the extraordinary.

There is a historical reason for Benedict's particular approach. Monks in his day looked to the Egyptian desert tradition of monasticism to find heroes. And heroes they were, accomplishing extraordinary feats, athletic in their intensity. If one monk knew of a neighboring brother who fasted three months, he would do six, and on top of a pillar at that! As romantic as all this sounds, the European monks failed to live up to the tradition of the desert monks. Instead they went to the opposite extreme, living lives of undisciplined license. Into this atmosphere, Benedict introduced his humane approach of zealous moderation, ordinariness, and balance.

The danger, of course, in proclaiming a lifestyle of moderation and normalcy is mediocrity. "Benedictine balance does not mean compromise; rather it is the holding together in one center of ultimate values, whose force we must accept not deny. What the Benedictine life can show us is the possibility of keeping equilibrium in the middle of polarity."[6] For Benedict, all activities, no matter how or-

5. Rembert G. Weakland, "The Role of Monasticism in the Life of the Church," *American Benedictine Review*, no. 32:1 (March 1981) 46.

6. Esther de Waal, *Seeking God: The Way of St. Benedict* (Collegeville, Minn.: The Liturgical Press 1984) 95.

dinary, are of equal value. Nothing is to be overlooked, because God can be found in all activity. Doing prayer, work, and study every day is important because we need the right amount of each. We need to hold up the polarities of body, mind, and spirit and find the equilibrium of God's presence in all three, and to do so within the paradox of zealous moderation.

PRAYER

Aside from legislating the structure of the daily offices, Benedict had very little to offer in terms of instruction about prayer. He simply assumed that his monks would have a time for private prayer daily, and urged them to pray all of the time in habitual recollection, whatever they were doing. Benedict demanded few words but strong and pure intent. "There are few practical directives given about how to pray and almost no theology of prayer. The general presupposition seems to be that prayer comes readily and un-self-consciously to one who does his best to implement the teachings of the Gospel in concrete behavior. The monk seeks God, not 'experiences.'"[7]

Prayer was not an activity isolated from other activities. Rather, the life of a monk was to be his prayer. Benedict was far less concerned about performance during periods of prayer than about the quality of daily life. M. Basil Pennington speaks of two Eastern religious communities near his Trappist abbey in Spencer, Massachusetts. Visitors often make the rounds of all three, learning a bit about methods of prayer at each. When they come to Spencer, "They ask: What is your method? I usually answer, the whole of our monastic life is our method. It is hearing the Word of God and keeping it. Whether we eat or drink or do anything else we seek to do all for the glory of God."[8] This should come

7. Michael Casey, "St. Benedict's Approach to Prayer," *Cistercian Studies* (1980) 328.

8. M. Basil Pennington, *A Place Apart* (New York: Doubleday & Co., 1983) 77.

as good news to those who have often felt that, in order to "really seek God," one must spend hours daily in terribly advanced forms of prayer. It is enough to hear the Word of God and keep it in everything we do throughout the day. Therefore, when one is dissatisfied in one's prayer life, the Benedictine method would be to look at one's life and deal with what is dissatisfactory there rather than to look for some new, better way to pray. Our prayer is a mirror of our life.

With "life as prayer" as our context, we are ready to look at those specific times in the day that the monk sets down as times "to pray." The most discussed of these in the *Rule* is the daily round of offices. Benedict determined that the monks would gather together eight times a day for corporate prayer. The offices mostly consist of the recitation of psalms, passages of scripture, and a few prayers. The purpose behind these frequent interruptions in one's day was just that: to interrupt one's momentum, to stop and remember God. This is a kind of legislated habitual recollection, in which, through frequent reflection upon Scripture as well as the act of coming together in the presence of God, one might blur completely the distinction between prayer and activity.

This is the part of *The Rule of St. Benedict* which is most difficult for non-monastic Christians. One cannot underestimate the compelling power of an office, for which the bell rings and other monks are assembled, waiting for you to arrive. For those of us "in the world," it takes a more internal commitment to undertake the discipline of the offices. It is not impossible, but there are certainly factors which discourage it. For some, a daily schedule of morning, noon, and evening prayer is simple to maintain. Others require some outside stimulus (such as the chapel bell for monks) to remember to stop the momentum of the day and focus on God. I carry around a daily office book with me, so that I am confronted with a visual reminder that says "don't forget, God is waiting." Frequently I also carry a small string of beads or a pocket crucifix to help me habitually recollect.

The use of the daily offices in Christian tradition is so widespread and so basic to Christian spirituality that it must be said that there is more to these offices than simply providing a way of regularly remembering God. The offices have at their heart the daily psalms and other passages of Scripture. The prayers are brief and, for the most part, also scriptural in origin. To regularly ''do'' the offices is, then, also a way of immersing oneself in Scripture. Prayer can get fairly uninspired, or worse yet, we can get ourselves way out on a strange and fragile limb if we rely entirely on our own emotions, thoughts, and impulses as our starting-off point. When one is immersed daily in Scripture through the offices, this danger is less present. We find ourselves continually returning to truth, to God's Word. The use of a prescribed system of going through the psalms and other Scripture is also a way of guaranteeing that we will not omit those ''uncomfortable'' passages. The use of the offices makes sure that we will encounter in prayer the totality of God's revelation, judgment, nurture, and teaching. Unguided personal prayer simply cannot provide this kind of wholeness and stimulation. ''We believe that the divine presence is everywhere. . . . But beyond the least doubt we should believe this to be especially true when we celebrate the divine office.''[9]

To engage in the daily offices or some other regular daily rhythm of prayer means also that we willingly enter into the monotony of repetition. Even if one uses the psalms or the Gospels merely as a starting point for totally ''free'' prayer, those same psalms or Gospel stories start looking awfully familiar after the first year. When I asked one of the monks at Christ in the Desert Monastery what it is like to do eight offices a day, every day, he simply said that ''it is relentless.'' Prayer can take on that quality, and the temp-

9. *RB* 19.1-2.

tation is to forego it for some other, more interesting activity. To succumb to this temptation, however, is to never have to encounter the self. As long as we look for "interesting experiences" in prayer, we avoid the encounter with God that comes in the midst of our ordinariness. God is beyond illusions and attractive signs. And so sometimes when we sit, not expecting anything, often in boredom, we allow ourselves to settle into the reality of what is, rather than what it is we would like. This is, I feel, the heart of prayer in the form of the offices or any other daily discipline of regular prayer: to settle into our ordinary life in God to the extent that we find a quiet peace there and cease to run after illusory idols.

The mainstay of Benedictine prayer life was and is the divine office. The place of the Eucharist in Benedict's own time is unknown to us, for his *Rule* does not really speak of it. Judging from inferences in the text and from other contemporary monastic practices, however, scholars feel that while the Eucharist was not celebrated as a part of the daily schedule, it was a part of the life of the community. "At most it is possible that a conventual Mass in St. Benedict's monastery was celebrated on Sundays and feast days. But perhaps Mass was celebrated less often, even without fixed regularity."[10] Whether or not the Eucharist was celebrated often, fairly early on in Benedictine tradition we see its inclusion in the daily schedule. Similarly, the Eucharist has become for many of us today an important part of our liturgical piety. While we may not participate in its celebration every day, the Eucharist makes whole our private and corporate life in prayer when it is celebrated.

The divine office and the Eucharist form the liturgical, corporate side of Benedictine prayer life. As a necessary balance, private prayer was and is a normal part of the monastic day. The spirit of Benedictine private prayer is simple, forthright, and in a form that is open enough for the individual

10. Adalbert de Vogue and Jean Neufville, *The Rule of St. Benedict* (Paris: Les Editions du Cerf, 1971).

to find one's own way. Benedict gave little instruction save that it should take place, and that one should pray quietly so that others will not be disturbed in their prayer. Over the years in Benedictine tradition, a simple structure of prayer has emerged, however, that retains Benedict's insistence that private prayer grow out of reflection on Scripture. This structure for private prayer is *lectio divina* or divine study, and its function is indeed study as well as prayer, for in Benedict's mind the two are inseparable. The form is simple: reading, meditation, prayer, and contemplation.

A full introduction to this way of praying is found in the appendix, so a simple explanation will do at this point. One begins with reading a passage of Scripture, moving into meditating on its meaning and relevance, and then offering up some kind of conscious prayer concern out of that meditation. Finally, one sits in simple contemplative silence in the presence of God. Each person, true to Benedict's respect for individualism, is free within this structure to pray according to temperament and the Spirit's bidding. Like the *Rule* itself, flexibility within a clear structure allows for individual growth in grace.

The daily round of offices and private prayer are the heart of Benedict's prayer discipline. These disciplines exist, however, for the purpose of supporting the most important element of prayer according to the *Rule*: habitual recollection. It is through praying at specific times, whether corporately or alone, that we are reminded of God's constant presence within and among us. And so Benedict insists in various ways that we remember God always: in greetings, in sitting down to eat, in beginning some task, or in whatever else we do, we are to continually remember the presence of our Creator. Benedict often uses intimidating images to bring this fact home. We are to keep death ever before us; we are to know that angels assigned to us continually report our activities and even our thoughts to God; we are to meditate on hell in order to stay vigilant in prayer and proper behavior.

All of this, I believe, is to give us that sense that in the here-and-now of this life is where we encounter God, not in some mystical place away from all we do throughout the day. Thanks to these (even intimidating) reminders, we get our priorities straight minute by minute. If God is watching us and we are going to die at some unknown hour, why not live right now as we are called to live? To pray as a follower of Benedict in the world is, then: to undergo a daily discipline of the offices or some prayer (preferably more than once a day) that is based on recitation of psalms and meditation on scripture, to participate in the celebration of the Eucharist, to develop an individual form of daily prayer, and to habitually recollect the presence of our loving God.

Readings in The Rule of St. Benedict: chapters 8-20, 52

Meditations:

How would it be possible in our daily schedule, if we have not done so already, to create a few minutes two or three different times to spend time with psalms and other Scripture?

What stands in the way of our being consistent about private meditative prayer?

Can we let go of the need to have some "wonderful" prayer experience and simply do the work of prayer, knowing that it will have its effect over time?

What helps to remind us of God's presence in small ways through the day?

Try to practice *lectio divina* as presented in the appendix.

STUDY

The use of study in one's daily life forms the second leg of Benedict's tripod. All three are interrelated, all three are necessary. Without prayer, study can become intellectually prideful. Without study, prayer can be uninformed. Without work, both can become removed from reality. Study is part of the necessary balance that brings the God-given use of the mind into both our prayer and work life. Through learning we understand why we pray, how to pray, and what kind of approach to prayer is most helpful personally and theologically. Through learning our work becomes more than mere work. It becomes our vocation as we grow in it.

Because learning is such an integral part of our being, Benedict legislated in his *Rule* that it take place daily for his monks. This gives study its proper place, for, as a daily discipline, what we learn becomes integrated into our lives. For many of us, learning is something we do all at once at a particular time in our youth—a fact which separates us from the continuing challenge of intellectual growth. Education becomes a mere tool to get us toward the goal of a good job, the favor of our parents, or social acceptability. Daily study, on the other hand, because it takes place slowly and consistently over time, gives us the much more desirable goal of becoming an integrated person in God.

Integration is key here, for the purpose of learning for Benedict is to become a better Christian. One is not to engage in study in order to become a good student—one is to do so in order to grow in God's grace. "What page, what passage of the inspired books of the Old and New Testaments is not the truest of guides for human life?"[11] With this purpose, the distinction between study and prayer becomes blurred. *Lectio divina*, as outlined previously in the section on prayer and more fully in the appendix, is clearly as much study as it is prayer. All study, if it is to be worth anything at all, must find its way into the core of our spiritual being where God can integrate the learning and transform us by his grace. And so when Benedict speaks of the use of Scripture and the writings of the Fathers, one is never quite sure whether he is talking about learning or praying. That is all to the good, for the two are indeed intertwined.

As a daily discipline, then, a follower of Benedict in the world today must view all learning in this way. Whether

11. *RB* 73.3.

one is studying advanced physics or the Book of Deuteronomy, the intent must be integral growth in God's grace. Whenever we use our mind, we glorify God who gave us minds. When we study physics, we come closer to the mystery of God's creation. When we study psychology, we learn how better to love and heal. When we study history, we enter more fully into humanity, God's people. When we study mechanics, we equip ourselves to make a better world for ourselves and others.

The study of Scripture and the tradition of the Church must have a special place in our growth in God's grace, however. In Benedict's time, monks had access to two types of material for study: Scripture and the writings of the Fathers of the Church. Scripture provided the revelation of God to mankind, mediated through man's interpretation and understanding. The writings of the Fathers were early Church tradition: further interpretation of God's revelation through theology, homilies, biblical studies, history, ethics, etc.

In our day, we not only have these two resources, we have a whole world of writing that falls under the broad umbrella of tradition. Everything from extremely obtuse treatises on systematic theology to popular devotional pamphlets is a part of Church tradition, because all of this is mankind's attempt to interpret God's self-revelation to us. We must choose out of all this tradition what stimulates our mind, so that we can grow intellectually and integrate what we learn in order to become a better Christian. Many Christians stop studying their faith at the conclusion of their confirmation classes. What a shame! Why shouldn't everyone who participates in the Holy Eucharist read liturgical history and understand more deeply the symbols we use, in order to enter more fully into the presence of Christ? We often think of such study as intended only for those who desire academic knowledge, but it is the experience of the living God that becomes known through stretching the mind. "What book of the holy catholic Fathers does not resoundingly summon us along the true way to reach the Creator? . . . For observant and obedient monks, all these are nothing less than tools for the cultivation of virtues; . . . Are you hastening toward your heavenly home?''[12]

Building a daily discipline of study is perhaps the most difficult of the three Benedictine activities for modern folk. Work is inevitable; exercise is socially acceptable; prayer is expected for Christians. But study is often looked upon as a luxury or an oddity for the intellectually inclined. Perhaps we need to learn how to be good to ourselves, and one way is to give ourselves the luxury of feeding our minds. Perhaps we need to look at how we already study on a regular basis and lift those times up to God as both an affirmation of the gift of reason and a way of growing in God's grace. Whether we use the offices or not, the psalms and other passages of Scripture should be a part of our daily existence. To reflect mindfully upon God's revelation in Scripture is to place our day, every day, into the context of living as a child of God in this wonderful, mysterious, and sacred creation. In addition to Scripture, we should always be working on some writing that interprets God's revelation. It may only be possible to read a paragraph at the end of a busy and tiring day, but one paragraph on spirituality or biblical study or the lives of the saints can be enough to expand our thinking and stimulate our spirit. All learning is a gift of our Creator. To mindfully, prayerfully, and regularly use this gift is to develop a part of our spiritual life—to integrate all that we are in God.

Readings in The Rule of St. Benedict: chapters 38, 42, 48, 73

Meditations:

In what ways do I already study on a regular basis?

When is the best time of the day for me to read and think?

12. *RB* 73.4,6,8.

How can I develop the habit of daily reflecting upon scripture?

What kinds of readings in the "tradition" of the Church do I find most helpful in terms of integrating my spiritual life?

If this is a new practice for you, for one week read one or two psalms a day and a passage or two from Scripture. Taking it a step further if desired, practice saying one or two offices a day. Some resources are the Episcopal *Book of Common Prayer*, (New York: Church Hymnal Corporation, 1979); the Roman Catholic *Morning and Evening Prayer*, ed. D. Joseph Finnerty and George J. Ryan (Collegeville: The Liturgical Press); or the full *Liturgy of the Hours* (New York: Catholic Book Publishing).

WORK

In *The Rule of St. Benedict*, work is placed in its proper perspective. It is not a reason for being, but rather a way of supporting oneself as well as a vehicle for coming to know God. All too often, when we meet someone, we immediately ask "What do you do?" as if that were going to tell us something about who that stranger is. Work has become our identity. This has its price, as we compulsively overwork and find on vacations that we don't have the vaguest idea of what to do with our empty time. "Vacating" is terrifying for some, and many who have the privilege of days off and vacation time find it impossible to get away from work. Further, we make self-worth dependent upon success or failure in our work life.

For many of us, to be able to love well is not enough: one must be making good money and be respected as a good hard worker. A clear example is found in the person suddenly faced with unemployment. In addition to the anxiety of looking for a means of support, the individual faces a real identity crisis. "If I don't have work to tell me who I am, then who am I?"

Benedict had a simple way of dealing with this problem. He knew that work did not define the monk, but that it was necessary and even good. Therefore the monk was assigned to do something, anything, in order to support the monastery and to have thereby an activity in which to seek God. But "If one of them becomes puffed up by his skillfulness in his craft, and feels that he is conferring something on the monastery, he is to be removed from practicing his craft and not allowed to resume it unless, after manifesting his humility, he is so ordered by the abbot."[13] This is not punishment for doing well, but a way of remaining rooted in who one is rather than in what one does. "Works of various kinds will be given him to do; but these are secondary, and no one of them is part of his essential vocation as a monk."[14]

A good example of this destinction between work and vocation is often found among artists. When asked what they do, one may find the reply: "I wait on tables for a living, but my 'work' [vocation] is painting." Vocation is a matter of our identity in God. It is who we are called to be in Christ. It is the activity through which God is made manifest. We are all created in the image of God, and each of us presents one facet of God's infinity. With this perspective, it is indeed possible to lose one's job and not lose one's identity. If one has a sense of personal vocation, then why not join the painter as a waiter in order to make ends meet? But if one has no sense of vocation, the fall is great. A kind of humility is required, and the Benedictine tradition provides us with a model. It is not so great a thing to move from one work to another even when it is forced upon us, as it is occasionally for the monk by the abbot. A sense of vocation gives us an interior security that no exterior insecurity can take away.

13. *RB* 57.2-3.
14. Cuthbert Butler, *Benedictine Monachism* (London: Longmans, Green and Co. 1924) 29.

The development of the activity of work in the Benedictine tradition is an interesting one. In Benedict's own time, the monasteries were clearly rural and therefore agricultural. Work was hard physical labor—a good balance to prayer and study. Not long after Benedict's death, however, invading armies sacked the monasteries, forcing the monks to migrate to Rome in order to be under the protection of the Church. And so, early on, the Benedictines began doing less physical work in order to support themselves. The balance of body, mind, and spirit began to be in jeopardy. Benedictines did, through the years, return to agricultural life, but in many monasteries with money, lay brothers (a glorified form of hired help) would do the work for the monks, who would then devote themselves to "higher things." This was in direct contradiction to the balance of the *Rule,* and later reforms restored the balance. There seems to be in the original intent of *The Rule of St. Benedict* a concern that good, honest labor would effectively keep the monk grounded, lest he drift off into intellectual or spiritualistic fancies. "They must not become distressed if local conditions or their poverty should force them to do the harvesting themselves. When they live by the labor of their hands, as our fathers and the apostles did, then they are really monks."[15]

This same need is ours as well. Some of us have no problem in balancing the mental and spiritual with physical labor if that is our job, but most of us need to create activities in order to use the body: gardening, housework, exercise. In our jobs we often more than fulfill the Benedictine practice of doing something useful and productive as a way of supporting ourselves. And so we have to do something other than our jobs in order to fulfill the other side of Benedict's practice of work: working our bodies in order to stay grounded and balanced.

But work is more than a way to make a living and a way

15. *RB* 48.7-8.

to stay balanced. For Benedict, it is also a way to find God. "First of all, every time you begin a good work, you must pray to him most earnestly to bring it to perfection."[16] Thus, our everyday activities as well as our prayer are rooted in the presence of God. Every activity is important in the *Rule*, important enough to do conscientiously and regularly. Work becomes, then, a way of glorifying God. Usually, when we think in these terms, we assume that God is glorified through our offering of "important," outwardly success-ful labor. While this is true, it is also true that dirty dishes washed well and in the presence of God also give glory. To do what needs to be done, humbly and simply, is enough. Benedict legislates that all monks will share in the common tasks of cooking, cleaning, and otherwise taking care of necessities. This points out another aspect of work in the *Rule:* it is a way of fully sharing in human commu-nity, human family. Without this shared responsibility in a family setting, people start to feel used and abused. When we do quite ordinary work, we join together with the lot of all humankind in living by the sweat of our brow. The Benedictine spirit of work is to humble oneself to do the ordinary, never to assume that one is above such things or the people who do such things.

And so we come again to a paradox: work is both unim-portant and very important. On the one hand, work is only a way to get food on the table; it does not define us. We can let go of its importance if we have a clear sense of iden-tity and vocation in God. On the other hand, every activity is done in the sight of God and can be done to the glory of God if done lovingly, well, and humbly. Work balances the activities of study and prayer, provides necessities, and fulfills the human need to take care of ordinary business.

Readings in The Rule of St. Benedict: chapters 35, 48, 57

---

16. *RB* Prologue 4.

Meditations:

Why do I work?

Where is my identity?

What would happen to my self worth should I find myself having to do something for a living I now consider to be beneath me?

Does my body get the attention it needs?

Can I see my ordinary work life as self-offering?

Do I share in familial, necessary maintenance work?

3

The Self in Relationship—
with God, Others, and Things

INTRODUCTION

In discussing the spiritual life, we are often tempted to speak only of the primary relationship between the believer and God. When this is the case, a picture begins to emerge that tends to disembody the believer from all that surrounds him, leaving only the soul and its sweet communion with the Lord. Nothing could be further from the picture painted in the Gospels, and nothing could be further from the life envisioned for and lived out by Benedict's monks. The Benedictine way is a way that is lived out in the world. True, many Benedictines are cloistered "away" from the world, but all live under a rule that recognizes the centrality of one's relationship to God as experienced in the world of people, structures, food, money, possessions, authority, and friendship.

Benedictines are not other-worldly but, rather, very worldly. While some traditions in monastic Christianity stress detachment and removal from worldly concerns, the Benedictine spiritual life is lived out in the midst of and through the world—the same world the rest of us experience. There is no difference between a monk and myself on this level. We both struggle with budgets, anger, responsibility to others, and questions about possesions such as "how much is enough?" Benedict gives very clear guidelines for his monks and for anyone seeking direction for living the spiritual life through, and not apart from, a life in the world. In this sense his theology is thoroughly incarnational. Jesus came into this life and redeemed it by his presence, and we must find God present in this life as well.

The sections that follow examine the primary elements of relational living: the self and God, the self and others, and the self and things. In all relationships, we see the Benedictine concern for balance. Balance is found between solitude and community, cloister and hospitality, the needs of the individual and the needs of the group, and appreciation for and detachment from things. This same sense of balance is crucial for those of us living in the world in a different, often more complex, lifestyle. Without balance, we find ourselves having too much time for others and not enough silence and solitude. Without it we have a clinging attitude toward possessions, and we find ourselves not only in the world but of it. Or we may spend an inordinate amount of time in isolated spiritual seclusion and become so detached that we are not even in the world at all.

This is why Benedict legislates the monk's relationships to God, others, and things: when he can talk, eat, sleep; precisely how much clothing he can have; how much time should be spent in prayer; what kind of process should be used in decision making in the monastery; and exactly how the kitchen duty should be rotated. With this kind of legislation it is possible that relations with God, others, and things will be kept in proper balance.

Over the centuries Benedictines have altered some of this legislation, but what has remained intact is a disciplined approach to living in the world. Those of us living outside the monastery cannot, of course, spend so many hours in prayer or possess only two cowls and prostrate ourselves every time we greet a stranger. However, we can, as we live in this world, learn to find a healthy balance of prayer, possessions, and relationships to others.

THE SELF AND GOD

There is a sense in which this section is redundant, for all of *The Rule of St. Benedict* is about the relationship of the self to God. But it is specifically the interior life that concerns this section, the place where we meet God in the core of our being.

The primary way in which we meet God is in personal prayer, and this subject has been dealt with. In addition to daily times of private prayer, Benedict calls his monks to what he terms "habitual recollection." This is more than the reminder that God is present to us at all times. It is an interior attitude about the self in relation to God that is carried with us day in and day out. This attitude is found most clearly in Benedict's teaching on the twelve steps of humility in chapter 7 of the *Rule*.

Humility becomes for Benedict the vehicle for learning how to be in relation to God. At first glance, this section of the *Rule* seems to be negative in the extreme, promoting an unhealthy psychology of being. Perhaps this is true. But there is still much to be learned. If we understand humility as the capacity for being grounded or earthy *(humus)*, then we can see that what Benedict is communicating is a way of being grounded in God. This being grounded is what enables habitual recollection, which in turn enables an ongoing relationship between the self and God.

Tolbert McCarroll perceives a healthy psychology of being in chapter 7 of *The Rule of St. Benedict*.[1] According to McCarroll, Benedict's twelve steps of humility include the

1. Tolbert McCarroll, "Humanizing Humility," *Benedictines* (1983).

development of certain psychological attitudes: self-restraint, surrender to God, patience in suffering, openness and trust, contentment, equality with others, obedience, interior and exterior silence. Humility is, for Benedict, a comprehensive psychology of living as a Christian in proper relation to God.

Another way in which Benedict develops the relationship between the self and God is through the insistence on a great deal of silence. Silence is legislated in order to allow the individual an interior peace—one in which a continual relationship with God can be cultivated. Benedict frequently warns against silly and unnecessary chatter, not to discourage enjoyment of life but rather to avoid mindless distraction. Living in the world, we will never experience a Benedictine degree of silence unless we live as hermits in a television-free apartment and never go out. But we can develop an interior simplicity by turning off the radio in the car, turning off the television, and avoiding meaningless socialization. Perhaps we are afraid of the silence that remains when we strip away the distractions, perhaps we dread the encounter with the self in God. Feelings threaten to overwhelm us, and we try to push them away with activity and company rather than expose ourselves to them.

On days off, I used to wake up in the morning with a mysterious sense of dread about the day. I would then plow ahead into projects around the house, social engagements, and attempts to entertain myself. After I became conscious of this pattern, I began to allow myself to be still. Feelings would indeed surface that had lain buried during my busy workweek. As I began to trust and enter into the stillness, a new kind of peace emerged, an interior attitude of silent contact with God in my inner self. The silence we so furiously avoid is often the very thing that grounds us in a life-giving relationship with God. To choose this inner stillness enables a shift in our intention. To accept it fully, fears and all, moves us into a new relationship with ourselves. Instead of living in our exterior, self-created self we find ourselves choosing to accept ourselves as we are in the moment. Being present to what is actually there is the only way to grow spiritually. We can fill ourselves up with all kinds of spiritual thoughts and practices, but until we are present to what is actually in the heart in stillness and solitude, we are engaging in spiritual entertainment.

Silence is legislated in the *Rule* as a spiritual practice or discipline. Spiritual practices are not an end in themselves but rather a means of growth in God's grace. The practice of silence is intended to develop the inner solitude necessary for this growth in grace. Without silence we are always outside of ourselves, involved in activity, relationships, and distractions. In the example given above, I found that I was terrified of silence and lack of activity because I was afraid of solitude. And perhaps I was afraid of solitude because of what I might find there: myself and God. In the end, there is only God and our soul, and in solitude, we are reminded of this fact. Our bodies give out, our relationships end through separation or death, we cannot take our accomplishments with us. When all is said and done, there is only our spirit and our Creator. Solitude brings us back to this basic truth. Stripped of everything else, it is much easier to see our life clearly.

And so, what do we find in solitude? We find all the inner demons and angels that we keep so carefully held down at other times. To pray in silent, empty-minded, contemplative solitude for an hour is a remarkable thing, even if undertaken every day. What a cloud of witnesses emerge out of the depths! Unknown feelings, fears, fantasies, and phantoms! This prayer of solitude is a kind of retreat in which we really get to know those demons and angels. It is easier not to do so, to be sure. But we are called to know God, and God is only known in the depths of our heart. We must plumb the depths of our own heart in order to find God.

Solitude, then, becomes an arena in which we confront these inner demons and angels. Solitude becomes the place where we work out our salvation with God, as Paul puts it. And it is hard work indeed. Chapter 4 in *The Rule of St. Benedict*, entitled "The Tools for Good Works," is his summary of those attitudes and practices that further our perfection in Christ. He closes this chapter with these words: "These, then, are the tools of the spiritual craft. When we have used them without ceasing day and night and have returned them on judgment day, our wages will be the reward the Lord has promised: . . . The workshop where we are to toil faithfully at all these tasks is the enclosure of the monastery and stability in the commmunity."[2] Although we may not live in a monastery, our own workshop enclosure is our hearts and the solitude that is found there. Benedict the zealot reminds us to view our spiritual practices as tools with which we toil in the inner workshop of the soul.

It is easy, however, to slip over from salvation by zealous faith to salvation by works. When we begin to view our spiritual tools and the workshop of our souls as the place where WE are building our salvation, we are in trouble. The one thing that saves us from a prideful attitude of "salvation by works" is the sure knowledge that all growth is utterly dependent on the grace of God. We are not capable of climbing to heaven. We can only do the preparatory work. But we can clear out the clutter at the foot of the ladder that God uses in order to climb down to reach us. The work is hard, but the outcome does not depend on superhuman efforts. Benedict, after cataloging all the activities and attitudes we must develop in the spiritual workshop, ends with this reminder and disclaimer: "And finally, never lose hope in God's mercy."[3] Hope is only possible when we hope in the success of God's efforts and remember that our efforts are only preparatory in nature. This is what it means to be

2. *The Rule of St. Benedict 1980,* ed. Timothy Fry (Collegeville: The Liturgical Press, 1981) 4.75-76, 78.

3. *RB* 4.74.

dependent on God and to accept and love ourselves as fallen creatures.

Readings in The Rule of St. Benedict: chapters 4, 6, 7

Meditations:

How do I view my spiritual practices? As tools to build my own salvation ladder or tools with which to remove the clutter at the foot of God's ladder?

Am I afraid of dependence upon another, even God? Can I give up control of my spiritual life?

Reflect on the twelve steps of humility as you can apply them to your own life.

Try to be conscious of the times you choose busyness over stillness and silence, and why. Choose stillness and see what comes up.

THE SELF AND OTHERS

Benedictine spirituality is unique in the strong emphasis it places on love in community. It is the primary vow of stability that defines the Benedictine community as a loving family. Here love becomes concrete and not simply a spiritual abstract. The monk vows to remain in a particular community of people for his entire life. The context of the monastery is family, and this is very deliberate: the monk will be have to deal with ongoing, committed relationships. The "other" will be there tomorrow and the day after that and the day after that. Relationships therefore have a singularly important role in the Benedictine way of life.

Healthy relationships with others are only possible within the context of one's own spiritual health. This is why Benedict places so much emphasis upon silence and solitude—to ensure not only that the individual monk will progress in his relationship with God but also that the community will be a healthy one. A parallel is seen clearly in the marriage state. When two who live in relationship do not give each other the solitude to grow as individuals, the marriage cannot remain healthy. Community is only as strong as its members. As close as monks are to one another, there is a kind of respectful distance kept between them. The same distance is essential in all human relationships, for it enables people to relate out of strength and maturity, not out of weakness and neediness.

Part of this respectful attitude toward one another in community is experienced through honor paid to one another as brothers in Christ. It is significant that the term *frater* (brother) is used ninety times in the *Rule of St. Benedict* and that it is used when speaking of the relationships between the monks, while the term "monk" is used only thirty times, exclusively when Benedict is speaking of general monastic principles. A monk in the abstract is a brother in the concrete. The juniors obey the older members "with all love and concern"[4] while "the seniors must love their juniors."[5] "In this way, they do what the words of Scripture say: *They should each try to be the first to show respect to the other.*"[6] This attitude may be translated directly to the family setting. All members of the family must be brothers and sisters in Christ, all on equal footing, all respecting and honoring one another. This is so much more loving than the hierarchical family model. Love in equality must begin at home, whether that home is a monastery or not.

This is why it has become so common for Benedictines to enter into issues of peace and justice in our world. They have grown used to seeing their fellow humans as brothers and sisters in Christ. A person, like Thomas Merton who lived under Benedict's *Rule*, therefore gets involved in questions about civil rights and the war in Vietnam. Many Christians see their faith as separate from their concerns about the wider world. For Benedictines, life is more integrated. All of life falls under the Gospel, and therefore equality and

4. *RB* 71.4.
5. *RB* 63.10.
6. *RB* 63.17.

justice in personal relationships must be sought out in political relationships as well.

Community life is a system that must be sustained in part by the organizing influence of rules and expectations. Issues of authority inevitably come up in community life, be it family, parish, or monastery. Benedict vests most of his authority in the abbot, but it is a particular kind of authority. One of the expectations of the *Rule* about the abbot's authority is that the weak, the old, and the infirm will be given special care. Heavy work is not to be expected, extra food is allowed, and the *Rule* may be relaxed. Without this understanding attitude about people, Benedict's abbot would surely emerge as a stern taskmaster. His *Rule* would have the quality of law. But this is not the case. The *Rule* is there as a norm for those who have the ability to follow it. *"Everyone has his own gift from God, one this and another that. It is, therefore, with some uneasiness that we specify the amount of food and drink for others."*[7] Charged with a great responsibility, the abbot's potential for misuse of authority is great and Benedict knew this full well. Parenting or any other kind of authoritative leadership has the same potential. In the *Rule,* the abbot, like a good parent or pastor, is charged with consultation of all before major decisions are made. He must seek consensus and peace. All must speak their mind and open their hearts to one another. Even the youngest must be heard and respected. Families ought certainly to take on this approach. Even the feelings of a three- or five-year-old must be considered if we are all equal brothers and sisters in Christ.

What does one do in community when members do not live up to corporate expectations, when they do not respect the authority of the group and its leaders? What happens in family life when children are disobedient? Underlying Benedict's response to these situations is always a loving concern for the offender. The rule of love supercedes the

7. *RB* 40.1-2.

Rule of the monastery. "The abbot must exercise the utmost care and concern for wayward brothers, because *it is not the healthy who need a physician, but the sick.* Therefore, he ought to use every skill of a wise physician and send in *senpectae*, that is, mature and wise brothers who, under the cloak of secrecy, may support the wavering brother, urge him to be humble as a way of making satisfaction, and *console* him *lest he be overwhelmed by excessive sorrow.*"[8]

But what happens when even this kind of concern does not bring about reconciliation? This is when tough love is called for, and Benedict knows how to apply it. Excommunication from the monastery is only used in extreme situations: it is only used after several chances have been given, and it is only done with a great sense of reluctance and loving concern for the offender. Further, it is possible for a monk to be excommunicated three times before he is finally and completely excluded from the community. Clearly here is forgiveness in action. Reconciliation and forgiveness are essential qualities of human relationships, everyone agrees, but difficult to exercise. How often we, in friendships, in parish life, and in the family, jump to excommunication as the first alternative. How often we exclude the offender out of a sense of revenge or divisiveness. And how seldom do we give the excommunicated even one more chance to return, let alone three. Benedict offers a loving, pastoral, and patient alternative for living in relationship when hurt occurs.

For the monk, love is not limited to the monastic family, contrary to many people's impressions of the cloistered life. An integral part of *The Rule of St. Benedict* is the relationship to outsiders who visit. It is not only assumed that people will seek out the monastery as a place of refreshment, it is also assumed that they will be welcomed and treated as Christ himself coming to visit. In a sense, there is no distinction between the love shown a brother of the

8. *RB* 27.1-3.

monastery and a guest. "We therefore meet Christ everywhere. This is the joy of our lives and the reason we feel blessed in the community . . . our hearts know only one love that is shed on every creature, because we see in all an image of the Christ we love."[9] Hospitality is a virtue that enables those of us outside the monastery to love more fully. Families, if they are to remain healthy, must love visitors as well, so that the Christ we love may be seen in all, and therefore our joy may be made complete. There must be a balance between the family's solitude together and their interaction with the wider world.

The community of the monastery, then, is truly a family. Love for others finds expression within this community of brothers through the way it handles authority, conflict, reconciliation, and in the ministry of hospitality. Families and parishes should find herein a healthy model or rule for their own way of being as well.

Readings in The Rule of St. Benedict: chapters 2-4, 27, 53, 64, 66, 72

Meditations:

What is my family?

What is my wider community?

How do I practice hospitality, and how does my love for others differ from love within my family?

What sort of decision-making process goes on in my family or community?

How do I handle those who commit offense against me?

THE SELF AND THINGS

We live in a materialistic society and age. To resist the sometimes overwhelming images presented through such me-

9. Guy-Marie Oury, *St. Benedict, Blessed by God,* (Collegeville: The Liturgical Press, 1980) 53.

dia as television, music, magazines, and shopping malls (not to mention peer pressure) is to place ourselves at direct odds with all that surrounds us. Living in the world, we cannot shield ourselves from these images as can those who are cloistered. Living in the world, we don't necessarily want to, either. Participation in the material world is a part of enjoying life. A brightly colored shirt, a good bottle of wine, a beautiful home, a catchy song or delicious meal—all of these are ways of being co-creators with God, a part of being joyfully alive. But how do we enjoy things without making idols of them?

The answer lies, I believe, in our attitude toward the things that surround us. Benedictine spirituality is thoroughly incarnational. This means that God is fully present in and known to us through this world. If this is so, we should treat the things of this world with reverence and respect. To be a mere materialist is to disrespect the things we carelessly possess and flippantly cast off. A Benedictine approach to things demands detachment: the monk must never possess anything that is not permitted by the *Rule* or the abbot. One does not own anything in the monastery; one uses things for a time. The abbot is to provide the monk with everything necessary so that there will be no need for grumbling. "In order that this vice of private ownership may be completely uprooted, the abbot is to provide all things necessary: . . . In this way every excuse of lacking some necessity will be taken away. The abbot, however, must always bear in mind what is said in the Acts of the Apostles: *Distribution was made to each one as he had need.* In this way the abbot will take into account the weaknesses of the needy, not the evil will of the envious."[10] Here is made a distinction between what is wanted and what is needed. If one has the attitude of detachment while having enough, then is is possible to respect, even to reverence things as gifts of our Creator. "It was typical of

10. *RB* 55.18-21.

Benedict to advise the Cellarer that the most humble equipment of the monastery was to be treated as having exactly the same value as the vessels of the altar. His view of the world implied no division at all between the sacred and the profane."[11] Things do not matter because they are not ours to possess, and yet things do matter because we need them and they can be used to benefit us and to glorify God.

The Benedictine approach to things, then, teaches that we are to seek God in all things, including our possessions, but to be detached from them at the same time. This is a sound theology of stewardship, and it presents a useful paradox for living in the world. A common myth is that the more spiritual one is, the more one will disdain the material. The fact is, once we truly respect the material and see it as gift, we are free to enjoy it. "As we look at monastic history, the monks who fled from the world usually found some of the most beautiful spots imaginable for the escape. And if perchance the spot was not beautiful when they arrived, it quickly became a kind of garden paradise. How can we explain this fact? Is it because monks who were disinterested in space and time could become good caretakers without destroying natural beauty? When one is detached from good, one can caress it without mangling it."[12]

Benedict, then, is not an ascetic who hopes to attain spiritual heights by hating what God has created. He is a worldly man in the best sense of the word, who appreciates and uses things with both reverence and detachment. St. Remegius, an early medieval bishop, is reported to have said while watching his magnificent episcopal residence burn to the ground, "a fire is a beautiful thing to watch."

This kind of attitude regarding our relationship to things brings a great freedom. It is at the core of the monastic tradition of poverty and, although not a vow for Benedictines,

11. Dominic Milroy, "Education According to The Rule of St. Benedict," *Ampleforth Journal* (Autumn 1979) 8.

12. Ambrose Wathen, "Space and Time in the Rule of St. Benedict," *Cistercian Studies* (1982) 83.

is definitely a part of their *Rule*. Benedictine poverty assumes that one will have what one needs and that the monastery will even possess beautiful things of high quality. But the tradition of poverty means that no one individual will own things, and nothing will be possessed that is superfluous. All things are used and respected both for their use and enjoyment. Dom Cuthbert Butler quotes Bishop Augustine O'Neill who was giving a conference on poverty during a retreat for junior Benedictines: "Calvary is the type of Franciscan poverty; but Nazareth is the type of Benedictine poverty. It was not the poverty of beggary, but the poverty that obtains in the household of a carpenter or other skilled artisan. It is simplicity and frugality, rather than want; and this is the spirit of Benedictine poverty and the type for Benedictines to set before themselves—the poverty of a workman's home, who is earning good wages."[13] Being "spiritual" does not necessarily mean going around in ill-fitting rags: "The abbot ought to be concerned about the measurements of these garments that they not be too short but fitted to the wearers. Whenever new clothing is received, the old should be returned at once and stored in a wardrobe for the poor."[14]

This is an approach to things that can be most healthy for those living in the world. Most of us are not called to live a life of intentional abject poverty, especially when we are child raisers and jobholders. We are, however, called as Christians to simplicity and frugality. All of us, if we are to follow the Gospel of Christ, must continually and honestly ask ourselves at what point we are making idols out of what we enjoy, at what point our possessions possess us, just how much is enough.

The Rule of St. Benedict provides some guidelines as each of us struggles with these questions. The limits of the *Rule* are designed to bring the freedom that comes from dis-

13. Cuthbert Butler, *Benedictine Monachism* (London: Longmans, Green and Co. 1924) 149.
14. *RB* 55.8-9.

cipline. The principle of having only moderate, ordered amounts of clothing, food and wine, and other things ensures we do not cross the line from detached use to destructive abuse. It is a freeing thing to go through one's closet once or twice a year and give to some charity those things that we do not use or feel frivolous about when we do use them. It brings freedom when we let go of a significant percentage of our income regularly for the benefit of the Church and other charities, most especially when that money would make the difference between frugality and luxury. It is a freeing thing to fast regularly, reminding ourselves of our overconsumption and others' need. Above all, it is freeing to seek moderation and simplicity in what we have and what we use. In this attitude we embrace the paradox of reverence for and detachment from the things of this created world. The incarnation itself is a sign of this paradoxical mystery.

Benedict did not speak to "social issues" of his day. He was concerned about running his monasteries. But with the explosion of information in our own day, even cloistered monasteries are informed about and very much involved in concerns of the wider world such as hunger, ecology, and justice. This flows naturally out of the Benedictine understanding of our relationship to things. To be a good steward means to care for this planet as well as for our brothers and sisters who suffer. To fight against materialism in the soul leads naturally to the fight against materialism and overconsumption in society. To care reverently for the tools of the monastery leads to caring reverently for the ecology of our world. In this sense, a Benedictine, incarnational view of our relation to things must be expanded to include all of God's creation.

It is a difficult thing to attempt a spiritual life while living in the world. The world we live in seems to work against much of what the spiritual life demands, and one area where this is most clear is in our relationship to things. However, where the challenge is greatest, so is the opportunity for grace. By God's grace alone can we expect to cultivate an attitude of reverence for and enjoyment of things, detachment and simplicity, and responsible stewardship.

Readings in The Rule of St. Benedict: chapters 31-34, 39-40, 55

Meditations:

Is my attitude about food, clothing, my bank account, and other things a resource for spiritual reflection?

To what am I attached and why?

What is my interior response to the cultural lure of materialism? In what ways could I simplify my relationship with things through moderation and discipline?

How does reverence and detachment affect my relationship to those who suffer, to my country, my world?

Appendix

A MODEL FOR A RULE OF LIFE: after *The Rule of St. Benedict*

Any rule of life should be developed slowly and very individually, taking into consideration one's own life circumstances. The Gospel can easily become nothing more than law when one rigidly applies an alien structure. And without the motivating influence of community, undertaking a rule can be difficult. Therefore, it is advised that one begin with where one actually is (in terms of spiritual practice) and add one new element at a time as one feels ready. This suggested rule is one I have developed out of my own life circumstances. It is intended to provide a springboard for reflection, and it serves as one example of trying to incorporate the spirit of St. Benedict into everyday living.

That in all things God may be glorified

COMMITMENT TO LIFE

STABILITY. A lifelong commitment to one's vocation, family and friends—being fully accepting of this life as a vehicle of grace.

CONVERSATIO. Openness to growth and change, willingness to look at oneself and to be challenged by God and others.

OBEDIENCE. Fidelity to this Rule and to the limits, demands, disciplines, and rhythms of the life we have been given.

LIFE IN BALANCE

PRAYER.[1]

- *Lectio divina:* daily morning meditation upon Scripture and psalms (can include the office of morning prayer but should also include silent contemplation).
- noontime office, meditation upon psalms, or prayerful recollection of the presence of God.
- evening prayer office, meditation upon psalms and Scripture or prayerful recollection.
- habitual recollection through the day.

STUDY. Daily reading in spirituality, also other readings.

WORK. One's job, Church ministry, manual labor, exercise, and financial giving for Church and other charitable work.

PRACTICES

POVERTY. Simplicity and moderation in possessions, reverence for and detachment from things.

CHASTITY. Worshiping God in the physical relationship, not using the other or abusing the self.

FASTING. A weekly two-meal fast of juice only, disciplined moderation in food and drink always.

SOLITUDE/COMMUNITY. Paradoxical but necessary aspects of the *Rule* that must be kept in balance within self and family.

ALMSGIVING. Giving a significant percentage of monthly income to Church and other charities, generosity with all possessions.

LECTIO DIVINA

St. Benedict did not provide a specific method of private prayer for his monks. In keeping with the tenor of his *Rule,*

1. For daily offices and readings, suggested sources are *The Book of Common Prayer* (New York: Church Hymnal Corporation, 1979); *Morning and Evening Prayer,* ed. D. Joseph Finnerty and George J. Ryan (Collegeville: The Liturgical Press, 1985); or *The Liturgy of the Hours* (Catholic Book Publishing).

he allowed each to find a way of praying that worked best for him. Through the centuries, however, Benedictines have develped an open structure for praying that allows for this individual diversity. Called *lectio divina,* it is based on the conviction that prayer must be rooted in Scripture as a way of letting the Word of God become a part of our inner self. It is not study so much as entering into the reality of the living Word, seeking its transformative power. *Lectio divina* involves the use of the body, the intellect, the heart, and the spirit as it moves from breath to reading, to prayer, and, finally, to wordless contemplation.

The method of *lectio divina* is divided into four levels: reading, meditating, praying, and contemplation.

One should try to set aside at least one half-hour a day for this practice. We move from one level of prayer to another as we consider the passage we have chosen, and as we do so the words and actions and faith represented in Scripture have a more and more profound effect upon our being. If we practice this method of prayer over a period of years, we find that we are truly living the Scriptures, praying them from the heart out.

Before actually doing the *lectio divina,* we need to prepare ourselves for prayer. The first thing to do is to get comfortable, sitting so there is a straight line from the back of the head to the bottom of the spine. Without tension, imagine a string attached to the top of the head that pulls the whole being heavenward. This posture is important, for it brings the body to attention. If we slump, the mind and spirit slump as well, and then we are not attentive to the Word. Some can maintain this position easily with folded legs, sitting on the floor. Many Westerners, however, find sitting in a chair far easier, or sitting on a firm pillow that raises one several inches. I use a small platform, about eight inches high with a slanted seat, kneeling on the floor and resting back against the seat.

Whatever one is sitting on, hands should be open, resting on the lap. Eyes should remain open and focused on something in particular. Some find a religious symbol— cross, icon, candle, or the like—helpful in focusing. Even a speck on the wall or the floor can help free the mind and spirit if one remains visually focused. Some find closing the eyes helpful, but I have found that this can result in too much imagination and distraction and can sometimes bring on drowsiness.

Become conscious of bodily tension and try to relax and let go of that tension. Go over the body in a brief mental check to make sure that the tension has been released. The body is now, in this position, attentive and yet relaxed— with eyes, legs, and hands open and receptive. Bodily posture is important, for we are one being that we arbitrarily divide into mind, spirit, emotions and body. If the body is present to God, then the mind and heart will more likely be present also.

To clear the mind and relax the body, the next thing to do is to become centered through the breath. The Hebrew word for breath, *ruach*, is the same word that was used for God's Spirit and also for the wind. In a very real sense, there was an understanding that our breath is God's breath, which is active in nature as well. The Jews also understood that when we die, our breath returns to God as it leaves our body. We are connected in this sense with all heaven and earth, with other people who share the same breath of God. Once relaxed and attentive in body, begin to pay attention to your breathing, knowing that God's Spirit dwells within you, that your life-breath is God's presence. This presence comes in and out; begin to lengthen the breath, on each breath extending it deeper and longer. A comfortable pause should occur before each new inhalation, allowing for a quiet moment of pure stillness. Try to use the diaphragm, below the stomach. This will allow for a deeper breath.

As you breathe this way, you may want to focus on a phrase which calls to mind the living God: ''Lord have mercy,'' ''My Lord and my God,'' ''Hosanna in the highest,'' or some other short phrase that speaks to you. Inwardly and silently repeat the phrase each time you exhale. Keep this quiet and intentional breathing going for three to five minutes, or longer as time allows. After we have prepared ourselves with the breath, we are ready for and receptive to the living Word.

1. Reading

A selection of Scripture should already have been made. As an example, we will consider Mark 2:1-12, the story of the healing of the paralytic. Whatever selection is chosen, it should not be too long, preferably a section that encompasses a single brief scene or saying.

Read the passage slowly and carefully to yourself, out loud if that seems to help. Use your thinking function to explore the ''who, what, why, when, where, and how'' of the scene. This is active reading, considering with the mind every angle of the passage. What friendship was displayed by the paralytic's companions! Why did Jesus forgive his sins when healing was what he seemed to need? Jesus remarked upon ''their'' faith, indicating that our friends' faith has something to do with our own forgiveness and healing. Why did the scribes get so upset? Note that Jesus did not have to hear their criticism of him; he simply knew it. Why did Jesus heal? Was it at least in part to display his authority as Messiah? When the paralytic was healed, what sort of reaction was generated in the crowd?

This is a mental scanning of the passage, intended to bring about an overview of the scene, which will help as we move more deeply into prayer. To use the mind is to pray. We are well underway already.

2. Meditating

While the reading of the Scripture primarily uses our critical-thinking function, meditating upon Scripture uses our feeling, sensing, and imagining functions. In meditating, we enter into the passage as if we were there, experiencing the moment for ourselves.

Let the mind wander over what you have read, and notice what "sticks out." It may be the size and intensity of the crowd, the anger of the scribes, the feeling of paralysis, the love of Jesus, or some other detail. Allow yourself to feel the scene: the sound of men breaking through the roof over Jesus' head, the closeness of all those people and the pressure on Jesus to do something dramatic, the terrifying amazement when a completely paralyzed man slowly stands up and begins to walk. Allow yourself to be there, imagining what it feels, looks, sounds, and smells like. One image may emerge as the dominant one. If so, pursue that image with your imagination. If it is the shock of seeing the unbelievable miracle of healing, then you might let yourself experience that shock for a while. In your mind's eye, look around you and see how others are reacting. Look at Jesus and see what he does or says, how he looks at you. Imagine what you might say to Jesus.

This is active imagination at work, and in doing this you may find that something quite specific to your life emerges out of the Gospel. Since the living Word is truth, this is a chance for your specific experiences to be touched by truth.

3. Praying

While all that has transpired up to now is prayer, this level is a way of putting thoughts and feelings into a specific intention directed towards God. In this level, we form the results of thinking and feeling into an intention of the heart. Out of the heart comes a prayer that emerges from reading and meditating.

Whatever emerged from the meditation, even if it is not emotionally charged or seemingly profound, is something that emerged from the needs and concerns in your life. If it was the shock of seeing the miracle before your very eyes, you may feel the need to pray for the grace to see the miracles of healing all around you. If your meditation focused upon the feeling of paralysis, you may want to pray that some area of your life that is locked up be freed. If it was the anger of the scribes as they heard Jesus forgive, you may want to pray for the grace to accept God's forgiveness of yourself or others. Whatever it is that came out of meditation, try to see specifically what in your life relates to that. Offer this to God in prayer, asking for direction or guidance, giving thanks or expressing penitence.

4. *Contemplating*

Contemplation is, for many of us, a word that conjures up impossibly holy prayer, the prayer of impossibly holy saints. This is not the case. Contemplation is simply being in the presence of God in silence and peace. It has been said that, while meditating and praying is looking at God, contemplating is God looking at us. This is where activity and passivity come together: we are actively watchful, expectant and open, yet not attempting to make anything happen. This is where we must be very vulnerable, trusting that God's will shall be done in us, and it shall be far greater than anything we could hope to accomplish by our prayerful efforts.

At this level, we move from our prayer intention into a sense of being still before God. Having thought, imagined, and prayed about the passage of Scripture, we have allowed ourselves to be touched by the living Word. The effect of that touch is what we take into contemplation. If you have meditated and prayed about your desire for healing of spiritual paralysis, take that sense of desire for freedom into God's presence. If you have meditated and prayed about your need to see the miracle of life around you, take that sense of miraculous wonder and simply be with God. Whatever it is, do not try to think about it anymore or come to conclusions about it or try to make anything happen. Remember, this is the point at which we give up our own control and allow God to work on us.

This is being vulnerable to God at the deepest level. It is not asking for anything in particular anymore, but rather opening ourselves as we are and laying that trustingly before our Lord. We do this knowing that whatever God does, whether or not anything happens, it is God's will. We will be transformed by God's grace according to God's will. And so we sit in peace, not expecting anything, not seeking anything. We sit in peace, naked before God and bathed in divine love.

To close the *lectio divina*, a simple word of praise and thanks is appropriate. Then, give yourself a minute to "reenter," sitting for a moment before standing and moving on into activity.

All of this may seem to be quite elaborate, but with a little practice it is in fact a very natural and simple way to pray. As we become used to it, we move organically from thinking to imagining, into praying, and, finally, being still. It is a method that has developed slowly over the centuries, shaped by experience and, therefore, proven in its effectiveness. To pray the Scriptures is to know the Scriptures in the heart and as an active force in our lives. It is being touched and transformed by the living Word.

The Reverend Brian C. Taylor's ministry as an Episcopal priest has included service in a small, rural mission in eastern Oregon and at Grace Cathedral in San Francisco. He currently serves as rector of a parish in Albuquerque, New Mexico, where he is developing a parish focus on prayer, enhanced by his education and lived out through service ministry to those in need.

Taylor's interest in Benedictine spirituality began with an association with the Monastery of Christ in the Desert, located in Abiquiu, New Mexico. Taylor is married and the father of two young sons.